3/
P9-AQZ-954

GROSS JOBS
Working with
FOOD
An Augmented Reading Experience
by Nikki Bruno

NRC   CASS COUNTY PUBLIC LIBRARY
400 E. MECHANIC
HARRISONVILLE, MO 64701

CAPSTONE PRESS
a capstone imprint

0 0022 0560187 1

Blazers Books are published by Capstone Press,
1710 Roe Crest Drive, North Mankato, Minnesota 56003
www.mycapstone.com

Copyright © 2019 by Capstone Press, a Capstone imprint. All rights reserved.
No part of this publication may be reproduced in whole or in part, or stored in a
retrieval system, or transmitted in any form or by any means, electronic, mechanical,
photocopying, recording, or otherwise, without written permission of the publisher.

Library of Congress Cataloging-in-Publication data
Names: Clapper, Nikki Bruno, author.
Title: Gross jobs working with food / by Nikki Bruno.
Description: North Mankato, Minn. : Capstone Press, 2019. | Series: 4D an
    augmented reading experience | Series: Blazers. Gross jobs 4D | Audience:
    Age 6-8. | Audience: Grade 4 to 6.
Identifiers: LCCN 2018036631| ISBN 9781543554922 (hardcover) | ISBN
    9781543559019 (pbk.) | ISBN 9781543554984 (ebook PDF)
Subjects: LCSH: Food service--Vocational guidance--Juvenile literature. |
    Food--Vocational guidance--Juvenile literature
Classification: LCC TX911.3.V62 C53 2019 | DDC 647.95023--dc23
LC record available at https://lccn.loc.gov/2018036631

Editorial Credits
Hank Musolf, editor; Bobbie Nuytten, designer; Heather Mauldin,
media researcher; Katy LaVigne, production specialist

Photo Credits
Alamy: RichardBakerWork, 12, ZUMA Press Inc, 10-11; ASSOCIATED PRESS:
Vaclav Pancer, 8-9; Getty Images: Dario Pignatelli/Bloomberg, 18-19, Nicola Tree,7;
iStockphoto: andresr, 28-29, BanksPhotos, 24, carterdayne, 13, davidf, 22-23, Fertnig,
cover, 1, FlairImages, 17, fotokostic, 14-15, IcemanJ, 8 (inset), Juanmonino, 25,
PicturePartners, 16 (inset), proibu, 4-5, thaloengsak, 18 (inset); Shutterstock: David
Tadevosian, 27, Kanghophoto, 20-21, Lamyai, 10 (inset), RossHelen, 6
Design Elements
Shutterstock: Alhovik, kasha_malasha, Katsiaryna Chumakova, Yellow Stocking

Printed and bound in the United States of America.
PA48

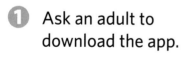 **Ask an adult to download the app.**

 Capstone 4D
Education

Scan any page with the star.

Enjoy your cool stuff!

—— OR ——

Use this password at capstone4D.com

food.54922

TABLE OF CONTENTS

WORKING WITH FOOD

Food can be delicious to eat. But working with it all day might ruin your appetite. Some food workers get covered in chicken poop. Some spread bat poop on plant soil. Others watch mystery meat squirt out of machines.

BUTCHER

No one gets grosser or closer to your food than a butcher. Butchers cut dead animals into clean, neat packages of meat. They use knives, saws, and meat grinders. It is a bloody, smelly, messy job.

GROSS-O-METER

DID YOU KNOW?

The United States is one of the highest meat-eating countries in the world.

PET FOOD TASTER

Pet food tasters make sure pet food smells and tastes good enough for cats or dogs. These workers look at the food, smell it, and, yes, even taste it. They also come up with new recipes. They use ingredients like liver and crushed bone.

GROSS-O-METER

DID YOU KNOW?

Pet food tasters have to chew the food they test. But they do not have to swallow it.

RESTAURANT HEALTH INSPECTOR

Health **inspectors** visit restaurants to make sure health and safety rules are followed. Inspectors have found dead rats and chicken poop in restaurants. One even found cat food in a refrigerator. The cook was using it in tuna sandwiches!

GROSS-O-METER

DID YOU KNOW?

Really good health inspectors can smell cockroaches. The bugs have an oily scent.

inspector–a person who checks or searches things

FISH GUTTER

The smell of one fish can be gross. Now multiply that fish by thousands. Fish gutters open and remove the insides of fish. This job is bloody and slippery. And the smell never goes away.

DID YOU KNOW?

Fish factory workers use little vacuum cleaners. The vacuum sucks out blood and other body liquids.

FERTILIZER SPREADER

Plants aren't very gross. But what they grow in can be nasty. Plants need a gas called **nitrogen**. Where do farmers find nitrogen? In cow, horse, sheep, pig, and even bat poop! **Fertilizer** spreaders breathe in the smell of poop all day.

GROSS-O-METER

DID YOU KNOW?

Some companies use human poop to make fertilizer. Machines turn sewage sludge from towns into fertilizer.

nitrogen–a colorless, odorless gas
fertilizer–a substance used to make crops grow better

CHEESE MAKER

Cheese is basically spoiled milk. Cheese makers use waste from **bacteria** to separate milk's solids from its liquids. They take the solid pieces called **curds** and cook them. The chunky pieces are pressed together into cheese.

MOLD: THE SECRET INGREDIENT!

GROSS-O-METER

Some cheese makers actually *want* **mold** in their cheese! Mold makes blue cheese creamy and flavorful. Cheese makers sprinkle some cheeses with mold. The mold gives it a white skin.

bacteria–very small living things that exist all around you and inside you; some bacteria cause disease

curd–the solid part of spoiled milk; they can be eaten or turned into cheese

mold–a fuzzy substance that sometimes grows on old food

CHICKEN NUGGET MAKER

Kids alone eat thousands of chicken nuggets every day. But few people love working in nugget factories. Ground-up chicken parts squirt out through machines. This mixture might contain muscle, blood vessels, crushed bone, **nerves**, and fat.

GROSS-O-METER

DID YOU KNOW?

Some fast-food chicken nugget brands are made of only half meat. The other half has other chicken parts, such as ground-up bone and fat.

nerve—a thin fiber that carries messages between the brain and other parts of the body

ANT EGG HARVESTER

Beef or beans are common on tacos. But some people in Mexico fill tacos with ant eggs! The eggs are high in protein. Ant egg harvesters have to collect the eggs.

GROSS-O-METER

DID YOU KNOW?

Ants attack the egg harvesters while they work. The workers have to shake the ants off without hurting them.

HOG FARMER

Millions of people love bacon. But they probably wouldn't love raising the hogs it comes from. Pigs are muddy and very smelly. They eat food called slop. Hog farms have huge ponds filled with pig poop and pee.

GROSS-O-METER

DID YOU KNOW?

Sometimes hog waste ponds explode. This happens after **methane** gas builds up.

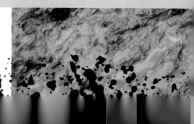

methane—a colorless, flammable gas produced by the decay of plant and animal matter

DISHWASHER

A delicious meal at a restaurant ends in the kitchen sink. Dishwashers must clean this mess. Imagine towers of crusty plates. Half-eaten food clings to forks and spoons. The smells mix together in a soggy mess.

DID YOU KNOW?

Restaurant dishwashers use strong hoses. The hose water sometimes sprays old food back in the dishwasher's face.

GROSS-O-METER

SAUSAGE MAKER

What are the grossest parts of an animal? You can find them in sausage. Sausage is a mixture of ground-up meat. Some sausages include blood and organ meats. The mixture is squirted into a **casing**. Some casings are made of **intestines**.

IN A WORD

Some sausage is mostly made of blood. It is called blood sausage. Blood sausage is popular in many countries. Each country has their own version of blood sausage. It may look gross, but many people think it's delicious!

GROSS-O-METER

casing–a thin, skin-like layer that keeps sausage together

intestine–a long tube that carries and digests food and stores waste products; it is divided into the small intestine and large intestine

THANK YOU FOOD WORKERS!

Food workers grow, make, and process the world's food. They often get dirty and smelly in the process. These people help us stay healthy and fill our bellies. They get gross to keep our food tasty and safe.

GLOSSARY

bacteria (bak-TEER-ee-uh)–very small living things that exist all around you and inside you; some bacteria cause disease

casing (CAY-sing)–a thin, skin-like layer that keeps sausage together

curd (KUHRD)–the solid part of spoiled milk; they can be eaten or turned into cheese

fertilizer (FUHR-tuh-ly-zuhr)–a substance used to make crops grow better

inspector (in-SPEK-tur)–a person who checks or searches things

intestine (in-TESS-tin)–a long tube that carries and digests food and stores waste products; it is divided into the small intestine and large intestine

methane (MEH-thane)–a colorless, flammable gas produced by the decay of plant and animal matter

mold (MOHLD)–a fuzzy substance that sometimes grows on old food

nerve (NURV)–a thin fiber that carries messages between the brain and other parts of the body

nitrogen (NYE-truh-juhn)–a colorless, odorless gas

READ MORE

Cohn, Jessica. *On the Job in a Restaurant*.
South Egremont, Mass.: Red Chair Press, 2016.

Duhaime, Darla. *Gross Jobs*. Gross Me Out!
Vero Beach, Fla.: Rourke Educational Media, 2016.

Gleisner, Jenna Lee. *Pig Farmer*. Gross Jobs.
Mankato, Minn.: Childs World, 2015.

INTERNET SITES

Use FactHound to find Internet sites related to this book.

Visit *www.facthound.com*

Just type in 9781543554922 and go.

Super-cool stuff! Check out projects, games and lots more at
www.capstonekids.com

INDEX